Food

by Rose Murray

How do plants and animals get food?

All living things have needs.
All living things need food.

Some animals eat plants.
Some animals eat other animals.
Some animals eat plants and other animals.

Plants Make Food

Plants need food.

Green leaves make food for a plant.

Leaves use three things to make food.

Leaves use air.

Leaves use water.

Leaves use light from the Sun.

Roots take in water from soil.
The water goes up the stem
to the leaves.

Green leaves give off oxygen when they make food.
Oxygen is a gas in the air. Plants and animals need oxygen to live.

How do living things get food in a rain forest?

A **rain forest** is a habitat.

A rain forest gets lots of rain.

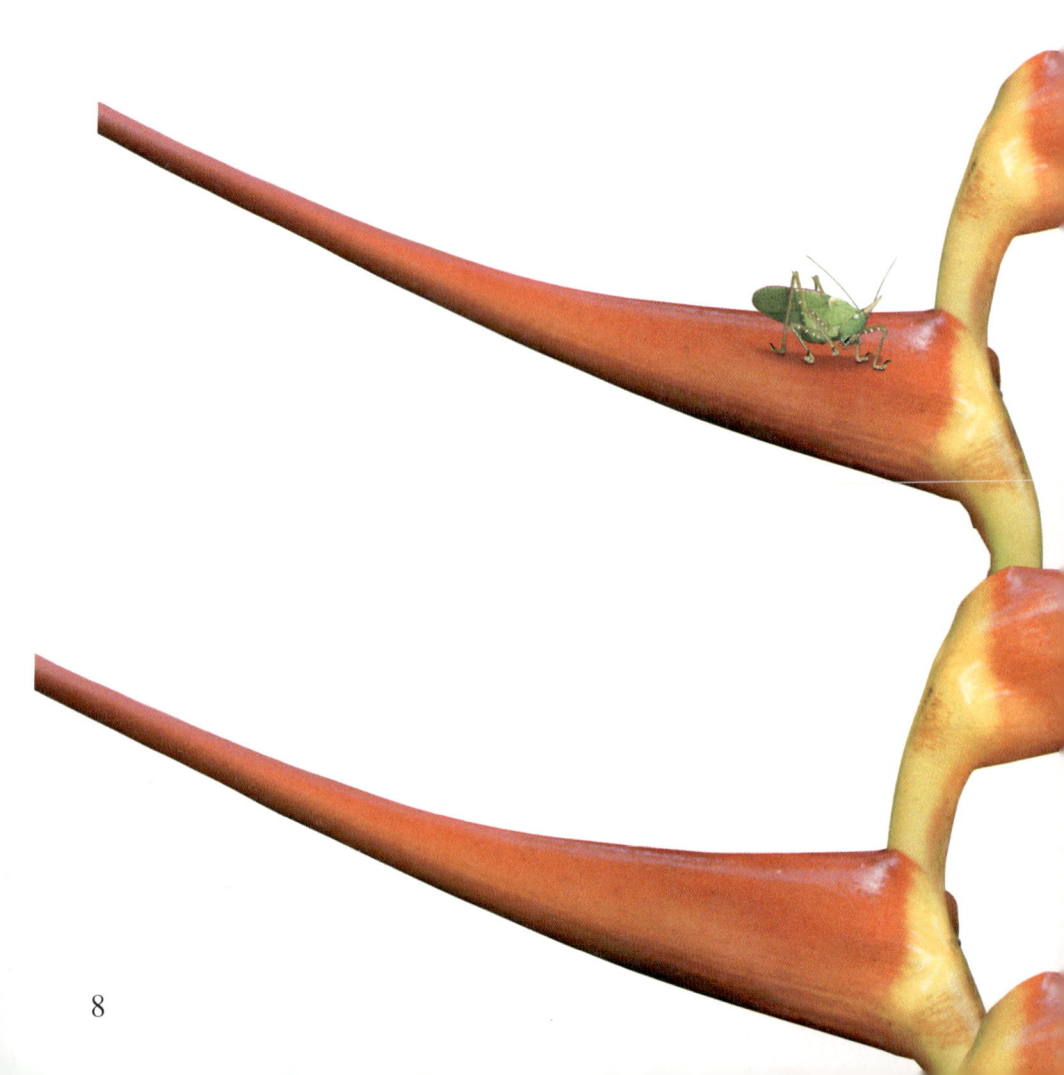

A plant grows in the rain forest.

The plant makes its own food.

An animal eats the plant.

Another animal eats this animal.

Food for Animals

Some animals find other animals to eat.
This is their food.

Plants make food.

Animals eat plants.

Other animals eat these animals.

This is called a **food chain.**

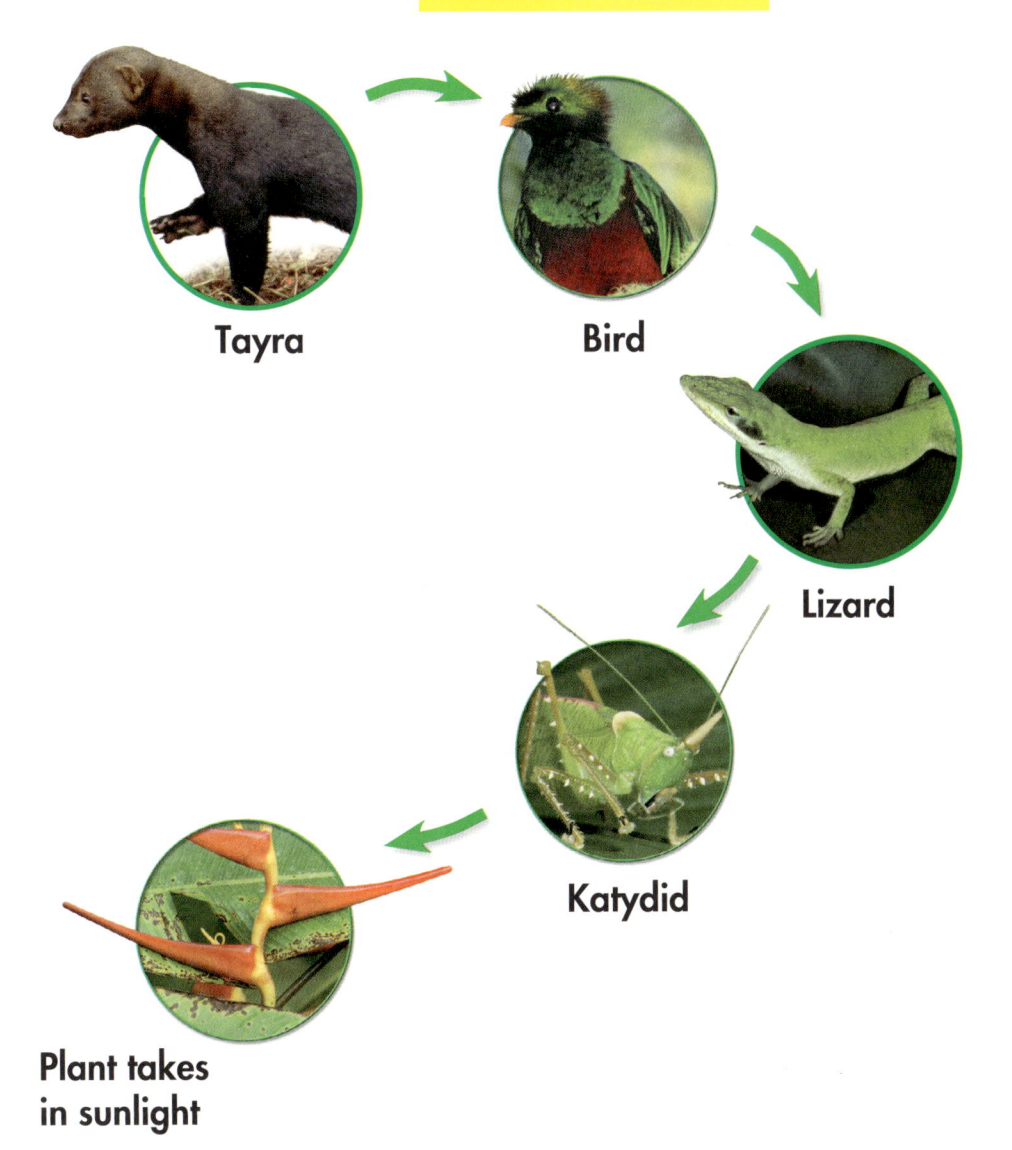

Tayra

Bird

Lizard

Katydid

Plant takes
in sunlight

11

How do living things get food in a marsh?

A **marsh** is a wetland habitat.

It is a wet place.

Marshes have food chains too.

Plants in marshes make food.

They use light from the Sun.

Animals eat these plants.

Other animals eat these animals.

Finding Food

Animals find other animals to eat.
A bird can catch a snake.
The snake is food for the bird.

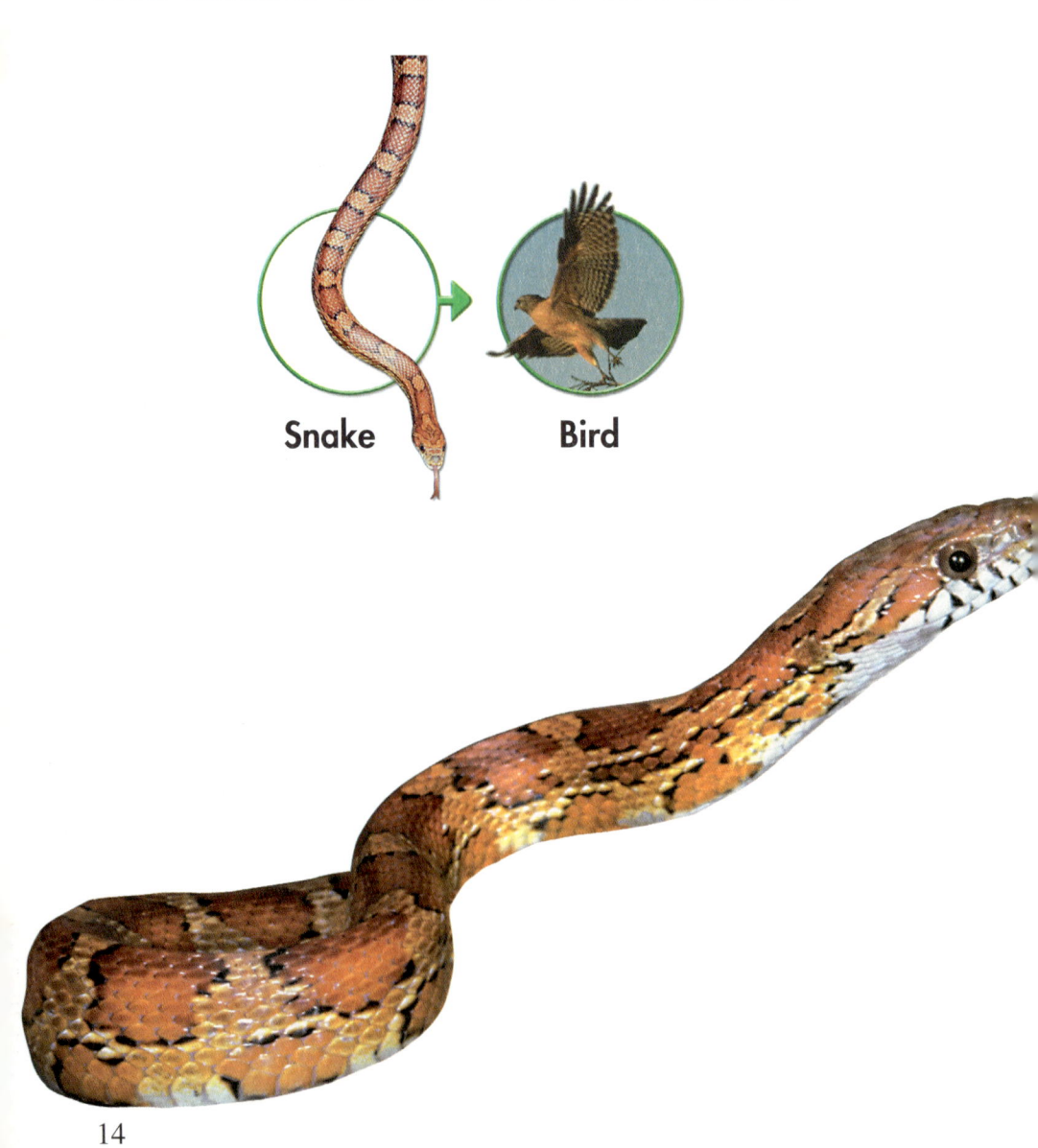

Snake   Bird

Food chains are in all kinds of places.
All living things are linked in food chains.

Glossary

food chain the connection between living things and their food

marsh a wetland habitat

oxygen a gas in the air

rain forest a habitat that gets lots of rain